THEODORE ROETHKE was born on May 25, 1908, and grew up in Saginaw, Michigan. From 1931–35 he taught English and coached tennis at Lafayette College in Pennsylvania. While on the faculty of Pennsylvania State College (1936–43) he published his first book, *Open House* (1941). A second volume, *The Lost Son and Other Poems*, written while Roethke was teaching at Bennington College in Vermont, was published by Doubleday in 1948. His third book, *Praise to the End!*, established his reputation among his fellow poets as an innovator, but it was not until the publication of *The Waking*, for which he won the Pulitzer Prize in 1953, did Roethke rise to the recognition of the general public.

From 1948 until his death in 1963, Roethke taught two courses at the University of Washington, where he was named "Poet in Residence" in 1962. During this period he made three trips to Europe, including a year as a Fulbright lecturer in Italy and another on a Ford Foundation grant, spent mainly in England and Ireland.

Words for the Wind, published in 1958, won seven awards, including the Bollingen Prize in Poetry of Yale University and the National Book Award. *I Am! Says the Lamb*, a volume of greenhouse poems and poems for children, appeared in 1961. *The Far Field*, containing the last poems of this great American poet, and published posthumously in 1964, won a second National Book Award.

Theodore Roethke

The Far Field

Anchor Books
Doubleday & Company, Inc.
Garden City, New York

*All of the characters in this book
are fictitious, and any resemblance
to actual persons, living or dead,
is purely coincidental.*

The *Far Field* was originally published by
Doubleday & Company, Inc. in 1964.

Anchor Books edition: 1971

LIBRARY OF CONGRESS CATALOG CARD NUMBER 64–12105
COPYRIGHT © 1958, 1959, 1960, 1961, 1962, 1963, 1964 BY
BEATRICE ROETHKE AS ADMINISTRATRIX OF THE
ESTATE OF THEODORE ROETHKE
ALL RIGHTS RESERVED
PRINTED IN THE UNITED STATES OF AMERICA

Poems in this book have appeared in the following periodi-
cals: *The Atlantic Monthly, Encounter, Harper's Bazaar,
Harper's Magazine, The Hudson Review, The London Maga-
zine, The New Statesman, The New York Times, Partisan
Review, The Observer, Poetry* (Chicago), *Saturday Review,
The Sewanee Review, The Spectator, The Times Literary
Supplement,* and *The Yale Review. The Kenyon Review, I
Waited,* copyright © 1956 by Kenyon College. *The Ladies'
Home Journal, The Young Girl,* copyright © 1961 by The
Curtis Publishing Company. The following poems appeared
originally in *The New Yorker: The Apparition, Her Time, In
a Dark Time, In Evening Air, Infirmity, Journey to the In-
terior, The Lizard, The Long Waters, The Manifestation
(Many Arrivals), The Marrow, The Meadow Mouse, Medita-
tion at Oyster River, The Moment, The Restored, The Rose,
The Sequel, The Storm (Forio d'Ischia), The Tranced,* and
The Tree, the Bird.

To Marguerite Caetani

CONTENTS

North American Sequence

THE LONGING

I

On things asleep, no balm:
A kingdom of stinks and sighs,
Fetor of cockroaches, dead fish, petroleum,
Worse than castoreum of mink or weasels,
Saliva dripping from warm microphones,
Agony of crucifixion on barstools.
    Less and less the illuminated lips,
    Hands active, eyes cherished;
    Happiness left to dogs and children—
    (Matters only a saint mentions!)
Lust fatigues the soul.
How to transcend this sensual emptiness?
(Dreams drain the spirit if we dream too long.)
In a bleak time, when a week of rain is a year,
The slag-heaps fume at the edge of the raw cities:
The gulls wheel over their singular garbage;
The great trees no longer shimmer;
Not even the soot dances.

And the spirit fails to move forward,
But shrinks into a half-life, less than itself,
Falls back, a slug, a loose worm
Ready for any crevice,
An eyeless starer.

II

A wretch needs his wretchedness. Yes.
O pride, thou art a plume upon whose head?

How comprehensive that felicity! . . .
A body with the motion of a soul.
What dream's enough to breathe in? A dark dream.
The rose exceeds, the rose exceeds us all.
Who'd think the moon could pare itself so thin?
A great flame rises from the sunless sea;
The light cries out, and I am there to hear—
I'd be beyond; I'd be beyond the moon,
Bare as a bud, and naked as a worm.

To this extent I'm a stalk.
　　—How free; how all alone.
Out of these nothings
　　—All beginnings come.

III

I would with the fish, the blackening salmon, and the mad lemmings,
The children dancing, the flowers widening.
Who sighs from far away?
I would unlearn the lingo of exasperation, all the distortions of malice
　　　　　　　　　　　　　　　　　　and hatred;
I would believe my pain: and the eye quiet on the growing rose;
I would delight in my hands, the branch singing, altering the
　　　　　　　　　　　　　　　　　　excessive bird;
I long for the imperishable quiet at the heart of form;
I would be a stream, winding between great striated rocks in late
　　　　　　　　　　　　　　　　　　summer;
A leaf, I would love the leaves, delighting in the redolent disorder of
　　　　　　　　　　　　　　　　　　this mortal life,
This ambush, this silence,
Where shadow can change into flame,
And the dark be forgotten.
I have left the body of the whale, but the mouth of the night is still
　　　　　　　　　　　　　　　　　　wide;
On the Bullhead, in the Dakotas, where the eagles eat well,
In the country of few lakes, in the tall buffalo grass at the base of the
　　　　　　　　　　　　　　　　　　clay buttes,

In the summer heat, I can smell the dead buffalo,
The stench of their damp fur drying in the sun,
The buffalo chips drying.

Old men should be explorers?
I'll be an Indian.
Iroquois.

MEDITATION AT OYSTER RIVER

I

Over the low, barnacled, elephant-colored rocks,
Come the first tide-ripples, moving, almost without sound, toward me,
Running along the narrow furrows of the shore, the rows of dead
clam shells;
Then a runnel behind me, creeping closer,
Alive with tiny striped fish, and young crabs climbing in and out of
the water.

No sound from the bay. No violence.
Even the gulls quiet on the far rocks,
Silent, in the deepening light,
Their cat-mewing over,
Their child-whimpering.

At last one long undulant ripple,
Blue-black from where I am sitting,
Makes almost a wave over a barrier of small stones,
Slapping lightly against a sunken log.
I dabble my toes in the brackish foam sliding forward,
Then retire to a rock higher up on the cliff-side.
The wind slackens, light as a moth fanning a stone:
A twilight wind, light as a child's breath
Turning not a leaf, not a ripple.
The dew revives on the beach-grass;
The salt-soaked wood of a fire crackles;
A fish raven turns on its perch (a dead tree in the rivermouth),
Its wings catching a last glint of the reflected sunlight.

II

The self persists like a dying star,
In sleep, afraid. Death's face rises afresh,
Among the shy beasts, the deer at the salt-lick,
The doe with its sloped shoulders loping across the highway,
The young snake, poised in green leaves, waiting for its fly,
The hummingbird, whirring from quince-blossom to morning-glory—
With these I would be.

And with water: the waves coming forward, without cessation,
The waves, altered by sand-bars, beds of kelp, miscellaneous
                                                    driftwood,
Topped by cross-winds, tugged at by sinuous undercurrents
The tide rustling in, sliding between the ridges of stone,
The tongues of water, creeping in, quietly.

III

In this hour,
In this first heaven of knowing,
The flesh takes on the pure poise of the spirit,
Acquires, for a time, the sandpiper's insouciance,
The hummingbird's surety, the kingfisher's cunning—
I shift on my rock, and I think:
Of the first trembling of a Michigan brook in April,
Over a lip of stone, the tiny rivulet;
And that wrist-thick cascade tumbling from a cleft rock,
Its spray holding a double rain-bow in early morning,
Small enough to be taken in, embraced, by two arms,—
Or the Tittebawasee, in the time between winter and spring,
When the ice melts along the edges in early afternoon.
And the midchannel begins cracking and heaving from the pressure
                                                    beneath,

The ice piling high against the iron-bound spiles,
Gleaming, freezing hard again, creaking at midnight—
And I long for the blast of dynamite,

The sudden sucking roar as the culvert loosens its debris of branches
and sticks,
Welter of tin cans, pails, old bird nests, a child's shoe riding a log,
As the piled ice breaks away from the battered spiles,
And the whole river begins to move forward, its bridges shaking.

IV

Now, in this waning of light,
I rock with the motion of morning;
In the cradle of all that is,
I'm lulled into half-sleep
By the lapping of water,
Cries of the sandpiper.
Water's my will, and my way,
And the spirit runs, intermittently,
In and out of the small waves,
Runs with the intrepid shorebirds—
How graceful the small before danger!

In the first of the moon,
All's a scattering,
A shining.

JOURNEY TO THE INTERIOR

I

In the long journey out of the self,
There are many detours, washed-out interrupted raw places
Where the shale slides dangerously
And the back wheels hang almost over the edge
At the sudden veering, the moment of turning.
Better to hug close, wary of rubble and falling stones.
The arroyo cracking the road, the wind-bitten buttes, the canyons,
Creeks swollen in midsummer from the flash-flood roaring into the
                                       narrow valley.
Reeds beaten flat by wind and rain,
Gray from the long winter, burnt at the base in late summer.
—Or the path narrowing,
Winding upward toward the stream with its sharp stones,
The upland of alder and birchtrees,
Through the swamp alive with quicksand,
The way blocked at last by a fallen fir-tree,
The thickets darkening,
The ravines ugly.

II

I remember how it was to drive in gravel,
Watching for dangerous down-hill places, where the wheels whined
                                       beyond eighty—
When you hit the deep pit at the bottom of the swale,
The trick was to throw the car sideways and charge over the hill, full
                                       of the throttle.
Grinding up and over the narrow road, spitting and roaring.
A chance? Perhaps. But the road was part of me, and its ditches,

And the dust lay thick on my eyelids,—Who ever wore goggles?—
Always a sharp turn to the left past a barn close to the roadside,
To a scurry of small dogs and a shriek of children,
The highway ribboning out in a straight thrust to the North,
To the sand dunes and fish flies, hanging, thicker than moths,
Dying brightly under the street lights sunk in coarse concrete,
The towns with their high pitted road-crowns and deep gutters,
Their wooden stores of silvery pine and weather-beaten red

courthouses,

An old bridge below with a buckled iron railing, broken by some

idiot plunger;

Underneath, the sluggish water running between weeds, broken

wheels, tires, stones.

And all flows past—
The cemetery with two scrubby trees in the middle of the prairie,
The dead snakes and muskrats, the turtles gasping in the rubble,
The spikey purple bushes in the winding dry creek bed—
The floating hawks, the jackrabbits, the grazing cattle—
I am not moving but they are,
And the sun comes out of a blue cloud over the Tetons,
While, farther away, the heat-lightning flashes.
I rise and fall in the slow sea of a grassy plain,
The wind veering the car slightly to the right,
Whipping the line of white laundry, bending the cottonwoods apart,
The scraggly wind-break of a dusty ranch-house.
I rise and fall, and time folds
Into a long moment;
And I hear the lichen speak,
And the ivy advance with its white lizard feet—
On the shimmering road,
On the dusty detour.

III

I see the flower of all water, above and below me, the never receding,
Moving, unmoving in a parched land, white in the moonlight:
The soul at a still-stand,

At ease after rocking the flesh to sleep,
Petals and reflections of petals mixed on the surface of a glassy pool,
And the waves flattening out when the fishermen drag their nets over
                                                              the stones.

In the moment of time when the small drop forms, but does not fall,
I have known the heart of the sun,—
In the dark and light of a dry place,
In a flicker of fire brisked by a dusty wind.
I have heard, in a drip of leaves,
A slight song,
After the midnight cries.
I rehearse myself for this:
The stand at the stretch in the face of death,
Delighting in surface change, the glitter of light on waves,
And I roam elsewhere, my body thinking,
Turning toward the other side of light,
In a tower of wind, a tree idling in air,
Beyond my own echo,
Neither forward nor backward,
Unperplexed, in a place leading nowhere.

As a blind man, lifting a curtain, knows it is morning,
I know this change:
On one side of silence there is no smile;
But when I breathe with the birds,
The spirit of wrath becomes the spirit of blessing,
And the dead begin from their dark to sing in my sleep.

THE LONG WATERS

I

Whether the bees have thoughts, we cannot say,
But the hind part of the worm wiggles the most,
Minnows can hear, and butterflies, yellow and blue,
Rejoice in the language of smells and dancing.
Therefore I reject the world of the dog
Though he hear a note higher than C
And the thrush stopped in the middle of his song.

And I acknowledge my foolishness with God,
My desire for the peaks, the black ravines, the rolling mists
Changing with every twist of wind,
The unsinging fields where no lungs breathe,
Where light is stone.
I return where fire has been,
To the charred edge of the sea
Where the yellowish prongs of grass poke through the blackened ash,
And the bunched logs peel in the afternoon sunlight,
Where the fresh and salt waters meet,
And the sea-winds move through the pine trees,
A country of bays and inlets, and small streams flowing seaward.

II

Mnetha, Mother of Har, protect me
From the worm's advance and retreat, from the butterfly's havoc,
From the slow sinking of the island peninsula, the coral efflorescence,
The dubious sea-change, the heaving sands, and my tentacled
sea-cousins.

But what of her?—
Who magnifies the morning with her eyes,

That star winking beyond itself,
The cricket-voice deep in the midnight field,
The blue jay rasping from the stunted pine.

How slowly pleasure dies!—
The dry bloom splitting in the wrinkled vale,
The first snow of the year in the dark fir.
Feeling, I still delight in my last fall.

III

In time when the trout and young salmon leap for the low-flying
insects,
And the ivy-branch, cast to the ground, puts down roots into the
sawdust,
And the pine, whole with its roots, sinks into the estuary,
Where it leans, tilted east, a perch for the osprey,
And a fisherman dawdles over a wooden bridge,
These waves, in the sun, remind me of flowers:
The lily's piercing white,
The mottled tiger, best in the corner of a damp place,
The heliotrope, veined like a fish, the persistent morning-glory,
And the bronze of a dead burdock at the edge of a prairie lake,
Down by the muck shrinking to the alkaline center.

I have come here without courting silence,
Blessed by the lips of a low wind,
To a rich desolation of wind and water,
To a landlocked bay, where the salt water is freshened
By small streams running down under fallen fir trees.

IV

In the vaporous gray of early morning,
Over the thin, feathery ripples breaking lightly against the irregular
shoreline—
Feathers of the long swell, burnished, almost oily—
A single wave comes in like the neck of a great swan

Swimming slowly, its back ruffled by the light cross-winds,
To a tree lying flat, its crown half broken.

I remember a stone breaking the eddying current,
Neither white nor red, in the dead middle way,
Where impulse no longer dictates, nor the darkening shadow,
A vulnerable place,
Surrounded by sand, broken shells, the wreckage of water.

V

As light reflects from a lake, in late evening,
When bats fly, close to slightly tilting brownish water,
And the low ripples run over a pebbly shoreline,
As a fire, seemingly long dead, flares up from a downdraft of air in a
                                                        chimney,
Or a breeze moves over the knees from a low hill,
So the sea wind wakes desire.
My body shimmers with a light flame.

I see in the advancing and retreating waters
The shape that came from my sleep, weeping:
The eternal one, the child, the swaying vine branch,
The numinous ring around the opening flower,
The friend that runs before me on the windy headlands,
Neither voice nor vision.

I, who came back from the depths laughing too loudly,
Become another thing;
My eyes extend beyond the farthest bloom of the waves;
I lose and find myself in the long water;
I am gathered together once more;
I embrace the world.

THE FAR FIELD

I

I dream of journeys repeatedly:
Of flying like a bat deep into a narrowing tunnel,
Of driving alone, without luggage, out a long peninsula,
The road lined with snow-laden second growth,
A fine dry snow ticking the windshield,
Alternate snow and sleet, no on-coming traffic,
And no lights behind, in the blurred side-mirror,
The road changing from glazed tarface to a rubble of stone,
Ending at last in a hopeless sand-rut,
Where the car stalls,
Churning in a snowdrift
Until the headlights darken.

II

At the field's end, in the corner missed by the mower,
Where the turf drops off into a grass-hidden culvert,
Haunt of the cat-bird, nesting-place of the field-mouse,
Not too far away from the ever-changing flower-dump,
Among the tin cans, tires, rusted pipes, broken machinery,—
One learned of the eternal;
And in the shrunken face of a dead rat, eaten by rain and
                                                ground-beetles
(I found it lying among the rubble of an old coal bin)
And the tom-cat, caught near the pheasant-run,
Its entrails strewn over the half-grown flowers,
Blasted to death by the night watchman.

I suffered for birds, for young rabbits caught in the mower,
My grief was not excessive.
For to come upon warblers in early May
Was to forget time and death:
How they filled the oriole's elm, a twittering restless cloud, all one
                                                                    morning,
And I watched and watched till my eyes blurred from the bird
                                                                  shapes,—
Cape May, Blackburnian, Cerulean,—
Moving, elusive as fish, fearless,
Hanging, bunched like young fruit, bending the end branches,
Still for a moment,
Then pitching away in half-flight,
Lighter than finches,
While the wrens bickered and sang in the half-green hedgerows,
And the flicker drummed from his dead tree in the chicken-yard.

—Or to lie naked in sand,
In the silted shallows of a slow river,
Fingering a shell,
Thinking:
Once I was something like this, mindless,
Or perhaps with another mind, less peculiar;
Or to sink down to the hips in a mossy quagmire;
Or, with skinny knees, to sit astride a wet log,
Believing:
I'll return again,
As a snake or a raucous bird,
Or, with luck, as a lion.

I learned not to fear infinity,
The far field, the windy cliffs of forever,
The dying of time in the white light of tomorrow,
The wheel turning away from itself,
The sprawl of the wave,
The on-coming water.

III

The river turns on itself,
The tree retreats into its own shadow.
I feel a weightless change, a moving forward
As of water quickening before a narrowing channel
When banks converge, and the wide river whitens;
Or when two rivers combine, the blue glacial torrent
And the yellowish-green from the mountainy upland,—
At first a swift rippling between rocks,
Then a long running over flat stones
Before descending to the alluvial plain,
To the clay banks, and the wild grapes hanging from the elmtrees,
The slightly trembling water
Dropping a fine yellow silt where the sun stays;
And the crabs bask near the edge,
The weedy edge, alive with small snakes and bloodsuckers,—

I have come to a still, but not a deep center,
A point outside the glittering current;
My eyes stare at the bottom of a river,
At the irregular stones, iridescent sandgrains,
My mind moves in more than one place,
In a country half-land, half-water.

I am renewed by death, thought of my death,
The dry scent of a dying garden in September,
The wind fanning the ash of a low fire.
What I love is near at hand,
Always, in earth and air.

IV

The lost self changes,
Turning toward the sea,
A sea-shape turning around,—

An old man with his feet before the fire,
In robes of green, in garments of adieu.

A man faced with his own immensity
Wakes all the waves, all their loose wandering fire.
The murmur of the absolute, the why
Of being born fails on his naked ears.
His spirit moves like monumental wind
That gentles on a sunny blue plateau.
He is the end of things, the final man.

All finite things reveal infinitude:
The mountain with its singular bright shade
Like the blue shine on freshly frozen snow,
The after-light upon ice-burdened pines;
Odor of basswood on a mountain-slope,
A scent beloved of bees;
Silence of water above a sunken tree:
The pure serene of memory in one man,—
A ripple widening from a single stone
Winding around the waters of the world.

THE ROSE

I

There are those to whom place is unimportant,
But this place, where sea and fresh water meet,
Is important—
Where the hawks sway out into the wind,
Without a single wingbeat,
And the eagles sail low over the fir trees,
And the gulls cry against the crows
In the curved harbors,
And the tide rises up against the grass
Nibbled by sheep and rabbits.

A time for watching the tide,
For the heron's hieratic fishing,
For the sleepy cries of the towhee,
The morning birds gone, the twittering finches,
But still the flash of the kingfisher, the wingbeat of the scoter,
The sun a ball of fire coming down over the water,
The last geese crossing against the reflected afterlight,
The moon retreating into a vague cloud-shape
To the cries of the owl, the eerie whooper.
The old log subsides with the lessening waves,
And there is silence.

I sway outside myself
Into the darkening currents,
Into the small spillage of driftwood,
The waters swirling past the tiny headlands.
Was it here I wore a crown of birds for a moment
While on a far point of the rocks
The light heightened,

And below, in a mist out of nowhere,
The first rain gathered?

II

As when a ship sails with a light wind—
The waves less than the ripples made by rising fish,
The lacelike wrinkles of the wake widening, thinning out,
Sliding away from the traveler's eye,
The prow pitching easily up and down,
The whole ship rolling slightly sideways,
The stern high, dipping like a child's boat in a pond—
Our motion continues.

But this rose, this rose in the sea-wind,
Stays,
Stays in its true place,
Flowering out of the dark,
Widening at high noon, face upward,
A single wild rose, struggling out of the white embrace of the
                              morning-glory,
Out of the briary hedge, the tangle of matted underbrush,
Beyond the clover, the ragged hay,
Beyond the sea pine, the oak, the wind-tipped madrona,
Moving with the waves, the undulating driftwood,
Where the slow creek winds down to the black sand of the shore
With its thick grassy scum and crabs scuttling back into their
                              glistening craters.

And I think of roses, roses,
White and red, in the wide six-hundred-foot greenhouses,
And my father standing astride the cement benches,
Lifting me high over the four-foot stems, the Mrs. Russells, and his
                              own elaborate hybrids,
And how those flowerheads seemed to flow toward me, to beckon
                              me, only a child, out of myself.

What need for heaven, then,
With that man, and those roses?

III

What do they tell us, sound and silence?
I think of American sounds in this silence:
On the banks of the Tombstone, the wind-harps having their say,
The thrush singing alone, that easy bird,
The killdeer whistling away from me,
The mimetic chortling of the catbird
Down in the corner of the garden, among the raggedy lilacs,
The bobolink skirring from a broken fencepost,
The bluebird, lover of holes in old wood, lilting its light song,
And that thin cry, like a needle piercing the ear, the insistent cicada,
And the ticking of snow around oil drums in the Dakotas,
The thin whine of telephone wires in the wind of a Michigan winter,
The shriek of nails as old shingles are ripped from the top of a roof,
The bulldozer backing away, the hiss of the sandblaster,
And the deep chorus of horns coming up from the streets in early
                                                                                    morning.

I return to the twittering of swallows above water,
And that sound, that single sound,
When the mind remembers all,
And gently the light enters the sleeping soul,
A sound so thin it could not woo a bird,

Beautiful my desire, and the place of my desire.

I think of the rock singing, and light making its own silence,
At the edge of a ripening meadow, in early summer,
The moon lolling in the close elm, a shimmer of silver,
Or that lonely time before the breaking of morning
When the slow freight winds along the edge of the ravaged hillside,
And the wind tries the shape of a tree,
While the moon lingers,
And a drop of rain water hangs at the tip of a leaf
Shifting in the wakening sunlight
Like the eye of a new-caught fish.

IV

I live with the rocks, their weeds,
Their filmy fringes of green, their harsh
Edges, their holes
Cut by the sea-slime, far from the crash
Of the long swell,
The oily, tar-laden walls
Of the toppling waves,
Where the salmon ease their way into the kelp beds,
And the sea rearranges itself among the small islands.

Near this rose, in this grove of sun-parched, wind-warped madronas,
Among the half-dead trees, I came upon the true ease of myself,
As if another man appeared out of the depths of my being,
And I stood outside myself,
Beyond becoming and perishing,
A something wholly other,
As if I swayed out on the wildest wave alive,
And yet was still.
And I rejoiced in being what I was:
In the lilac change, the white reptilian calm,
In the bird beyond the bough, the single one
With all the air to greet him as he flies,
The dolphin rising from the darkening waves;

And in this rose, this rose in the sea-wind,
Rooted in stone, keeping the whole of light,
Gathering to itself sound and silence—
Mine and the sea-wind's.

Love Poems

THE YOUNG GIRL

What can the spirit believe?—
It takes in the whole body;
I, on coming to love,
Make that my study.

We are one, and yet we are more,
I am told by those who know,—
At times content to be two.
Today I skipped on the shore,
My eyes neither here nor there,
My thin arms to and fro,
A bird my body,
My bird-blood ready.

HER WORDS

A young mouth laughs at a gift.
She croons, like a cat to its claws;
Cries, 'I'm old enough to live
And delight in a lover's praise,
Yet keep to myself my own mind;
I dance to the right, to the left;
My luck raises the wind.'

'Write all my whispers down,'
She cries to her true love.
'I believe, I believe, in the moon!—
What weather of heaven is this?'

'The storm, the storm of a kiss.'

THE APPARITION

My pillow won't tell me
    Where he has gone,
The soft-footed one
    Who passed by, alone.

Who took my heart, whole,
    With a tilt of his eye,
And with it, my soul,
    And it like to die.

I twist, and I turn,
    My breath but a sigh.
Dare I grieve? Dare I mourn?
    He walks by. He walks by.

HER RETICENCE

If I could send him only
One sleeve with my hand in it,
Disembodied, unbloody,
For him to kiss or caress
As he would or would not,—
But never the full look of my eyes,
Nor the whole heart of my thought,
Nor the soul haunting my body,
Nor my lips, my breasts, my thighs
That shiver in the wind
When the wind sighs.

HER LONGING

Before this longing,
I lived serene as a fish,
At one with the plants in the pond,
The mare's tail, the floating frogbit,
Among my eight-legged friends,
Open like a pool, a lesser parsnip,
Like a leech, looping myself along,
A bug-eyed edible one,
A mouth like a stickleback,—
A thing quiescent!

But now—
The wild stream, the sea itself cannot contain me:
I dive with the black hag, the cormorant,
Or walk the pebbly shore with the humpbacked heron,
Shaking out my catch in the morning sunlight,
Or rise with the gar-eagle, the great-winged condor,
Floating over the mountains,
Pitting my breast against the rushing air,
A phoenix, sure of my body,
Perpetually rising out of myself,
My wings hovering over the shorebirds,
Or beating against the black clouds of the storm,
Protecting the sea-cliffs.

HER TIME

When all
My waterfall
Fancies sway away
From me, in the sea's silence;
In the time
When the tide moves
Neither forward nor back,
And the small waves
Begin rising whitely,
And the quick winds
Flick over the close whitecaps,
And two scoters fly low,
Their four wings beating together,
And my salt-laden hair
Flies away from my face
Before the almost invisible
Spray, and the small shapes
Of light on the far
Cliff disappear in a last
Glint of the sun, before
The long surf of the storm booms
Down on the near shore,
When everything—birds, men, dogs—
Runs to cover:
I'm one to follow,
To follow.

SONG

My wrath, where's the edge
Of the fine shapely thought
That I carried so long
When so young, when so young?

My rage, what's to be
The soul's privilege?
Will the heart eat the heart?
What's to come? What's to come?

O love, you who hear
The slow tick of time
In your sea-buried ear,
Tell me now, tell me now.

LIGHT LISTENED

O what could be more nice   *A*
Than her ways with a man? *B*
She kissed me more than twice *A*
Once we were left alone. *C*
Who'd look when he could feel? *D*
She'd more sides than a seal. *D*

The close air faintly stirred. *E*
Light deepened to a bell, *F*
The love-beat of a bird. *E*
She kept her body still *G*
And watched the weather flow. *H*
We live by what we do. *I*

All's known, all, all around:
The shape of things to be;
A green thing loves the green
And loves the living ground.
The deep shade gathers night;
She changed with changing light.

We met to leave again
The time we broke from time;
A cold air brought its rain,
The singing of a stem.
She sang a final song;
Light listened when she sang.

THE HAPPY THREE

Inside, my darling wife
Sharpened a butcher knife;
Sighed out her pure relief
    That I was gone.

When I had tried to clean
My papers up, between
Words skirting the obscene—
    She frowned her frown.

Shelves have a special use;
And Why muddy shoes
In with your underclothes?
    She asked, woman.

So I betook myself
With not one tiny laugh
To drink some half-and-half
    On the back lawn.

Who should come up right then,
But our goose, Marianne,
Having escaped her pen,
    Hunting the sun.

Named for a poetess,
(Whom I like none-the-less),
Her pure-white featheriness
    She paused to preen;

But when she pecked my toe,
My banked-up vertigo
Vanished like April snow;
    All rage was gone.

Then a close towhee, a
Phoebe not far away
Sang out audaciously
    Notes finely drawn.

Back to the house we ran,
Me, and dear Marianne—
Then we romped out again,
      Out again,
      Out again,
    Three in the sun.

HIS FOREBODING

I

The shoal rocks with the sea.
I, living, still abide
The incommensurate dread
Of being, being away
From one comely head.

II

Thought upon thought can be
A burden to the soul.
Who knows the end of it all?
When I pause to talk to a stone,
The dew draws near.

III

I sing the wind around
And hear myself return
To nothingness, alone.
The loneliest thing I know
Is my own mind at play.

IV

Is she the all of light?
I sniff the darkening air
And listen to my own feet.
A storm's increasing where
The winds and waters meet.

THE SHY MAN

The full moon was shining upon the broad sea;   *A*
I sang to the one star that looked down at me;   *A*
I sang to the white horse that grazed on the quay,—   *B*
    As I walked by the high sea-wall.   *C*
      But my lips they,   *B*
      My lips they,   *B*
    Said never a word,   *D*
    As I moped by the high sea-wall.   *C*

refrain

The curlew's slow night song came on the water.
That tremble of sweet notes set my heart astir,
As I walked beside her, the O'Connell's daughter,
    I knew that I did love her.
      But my lips they,
      My lips they,
    Said never a word,
    As we walked by the high sea-wall.

The full moon has fallen, the night wind is down
And I lie here thinking in bleak Bofin town
I lie here and thinking, 'I am not alone.'
    For here close beside me is O'Connell's daughter,
      And my lips they, my lips they,
      Say many a word,
    As we embrace by the high sea-wall.
      O! my lips they, my lips they,
      Say many a word,
    As we kiss by the high sea-wall.

HER WRATH

Dante himself endured,
And purgatorial ire;
I, who renew the fire,
Shiver, and more than twice,
From another Beatrice.

WISH FOR A YOUNG WIFE

My lizard, my lively writher,
May your limbs never wither,
May the eyes in your face
Survive the green ice
Of envy's mean gaze;
May you live out your life
Without hate, without grief,
And your hair ever blaze,
In the sun, in the sun,
When I am undone,
When I am no one.

Mixed Sequence

THE ABYSS

I

Is the stair here?
Where's the stair?
'The stair's right there,
But it goes nowhere.'

And the abyss? the abyss?
'The abyss you can't miss:
It's right where you are—
A step down the stair.'

    Each time ever
    There always is
    Noon of failure,
    Part of a house.

    In the middle of,
    Around a cloud,
    On top a thistle
    The wind's slowing.

II

I have been spoken to variously
But heard little.
My inward witness is dismayed
By my unguarded mouth.
I have taken, too often, the dangerous path,
The vague, the arid,
Neither in nor out of this life.

Among us, who is holy?
What speech abides?
I hear the noise of the wall.
They have declared themselves,
Those who despise the dove.

Be with me, Whitman, maker of catalogues:
For the world invades me again,
And once more the tongues begin babbling.
And the terrible hunger for objects quails me:
The sill trembles.
And there on the blind
A furred caterpillar crawls down a string.
My symbol!
For I have moved closer to death, lived with death;
Like a nurse he sat with me for weeks, a sly surly attendant,
Watching my hands, wary.
Who sent him away?
I'm no longer a bird dipping a beak into rippling water
But a mole winding through earth,
A night-fishing otter.

III

Too much reality can be a dazzle, a surfeit;
Too close immediacy an exhaustion:
As when the door swings open in a florist's storeroom—
The rush of smells strikes like a cold fire, the throat freezes,
And we turn back to the heat of August,
Chastened.

So the abyss—
The slippery cold heights,
After the blinding misery,
The climbing, the endless turning,
Strike like a fire,
A terrible violence of creation,
A flash into the burning heart of the abominable;

Yet if we wait, unafraid, beyond the fearful instant,
The burning lake turns into a forest pool,
The fire subsides into rings of water,
A sunlit silence.

IV

How can I dream except beyond this life?
Can I outleap the sea—
The edge of all the land, the final sea?
I envy the tendrils, their eyeless seeking,
The child's hand reaching into the coiled smilax,
And I obey the wind at my back
Bringing me home from the twilight fishing.

In this, my half-rest,
Knowing slows for a moment,
And not-knowing enters, silent,
Bearing being itself,
And the fire dances
To the stream's
Flowing.

Do we move toward God, or merely another condition?
By the salt waves I hear a river's undersong,
In a place of mottled clouds, a thin mist morning and evening.
I rock between dark and dark,
My soul nearly my own,
My dead selves singing.
And I embrace this calm—
Such quiet under the small leaves!—
Near the stem, whiter at root,
A luminous stillness.

The shade speaks slowly:
'Adore and draw near.
Who knows this—
Knows all.'

V

I thirst by day. I watch by night.
I receive! I have been received!
I hear the flowers drinking in their light,
I have taken counsel of the crab and the sea-urchin,
I recall the falling of small waters,
The stream slipping beneath the mossy logs,
Winding down to the stretch of irregular sand,
The great logs piled like matchsticks.

I am most immoderately married:
The Lord God has taken my heaviness away;
I have merged, like the bird, with the bright air,
And my thought flies to the place by the bo-tree.

Being, not doing, is my first joy.

ELEGY

Her face like a rain-beaten stone on the day she rolled off
With the dark hearse, and enough flowers for an alderman,—
And so she was, in her way, Aunt Tilly.

Sighs, sighs, who says they have sequence?
Between the spirit and the flesh,—what war?
She never knew;
For she asked no quarter and gave none,
Who sat with the dead when the relatives left,
Who fed and tended the infirm, the mad, the epileptic,
And, with a harsh rasp of a laugh at herself,
Faced up to the worst.

I recall how she harried the children away all the late summer
From the one beautiful thing in her yard, the peachtree;
How she kept the wizened, the fallen, the misshapen for herself,
And picked and pickled the best, to be left on rickety doorsteps.

And yet she died in agony,
Her tongue, at the last, thick, black as an ox's.

Terror of cops, bill collectors, betrayers of the poor,—
I see you in some celestial supermarket,
Moving serenely among the leeks and cabbages,
Probing the squash,
Bearing down, with two steady eyes,
On the quaking butcher.

OTTO

I

He was the youngest son of a strange brood,
A Prussian who learned early to be rude
To fools and frauds: He does not put on airs
Who lived above a potting shed for years.
I think of him, and I think of his men,
As close to him as any kith or kin.
Max Laurisch had the greenest thumb of all.
A florist does not woo the beautiful:
He potted plants as if he hated them.
What root of his ever denied its stem?
When flowers grew, their bloom extended him.

II

His hand could fit into a woman's glove,
And in a wood he knew whatever moved;
Once when he saw two poachers on his land,
He threw his rifle over with one hand;
Dry bark flew in their faces from his shot,—
He always knew what he was aiming at.
They stood there with their guns; he walked toward,
Without his rifle, and slapped each one hard;
It was no random act, for those two men
Had slaughtered game, and cut young fir trees down.
I was no more than seven at the time.

III

A house for flowers! House upon house they built,
Whether for love or out of obscure guilt
For ancestors who loved a warlike show,
Or Frenchmen killed a hundred years ago,
And yet still violent men, whose stacked-up guns
Killed every cat that neared their pheasant runs;
When Hattie Wright's angora died as well,
My father took it to her, by the tail.
Who loves the small can be both saint and boor,
(And some grow out of shape, their seed impure;)
The Indians loved him, and the Polish poor.

IV

In my mind's eye I see those fields of glass,
As I looked out at them from the high house,
Riding beneath the moon, hid from the moon,
Then slowly breaking whiter in the dawn;
When George the watchman's lantern dropped from sight
The long pipes knocked: it was the end of night.
I'd stand upon my bed, a sleepless child
Watching the waking of my father's world.—
O world so far away! O my lost world!

THE CHUMS

Some are in prison; some are dead;
 And none has read my books,
And yet my thought turns back to them,
 And I remember looks

Their sisters gave me, once or twice;
 But when I slowed my feet,
They taught me not to be too nice
 The way I tipped my hat.

And when I slipped upon the ice,
They saw that I fell more than twice.
 I'm grateful for that.

THE LIZARD

He too has eaten well—
I can see that by the distended pulsing middle;
And his world and mine are the same,
The Mediterranean sun shining on us, equally,
His head, stiff as a scarab, turned to one side,
His right eye staring straight at me,
One leaf-like foot hung laxly
Over the worn curb of the terrace,
The tail straight as an awl,
Then suddenly flung up and over,
Ending curled around and over again,
A thread-like firmness.

(Would a cigarette disturb him?)

At the first scratch of the match
He turns his head slightly,
Retiring to nudge his neck half-way under
A dried strawberry leaf,
His tail gray with the ground now,
One round eye still toward me.
A white cabbage-butterfly drifts in,
Bumbling up and around the bamboo windbreak;
But the eye of the tiny lizard stays with me.
One greenish lid lifts a bit higher,
Then slides down over the eye's surface,
Rising again, slowly,
Opening, closing.

To whom does this terrace belong?—
With its limestone crumbling into fine grayish dust,
Its bevy of bees, and its wind-beaten rickety sun-chairs.
Not to me, but this lizard,
Older than I, or the cockroach.

[59]

THE MEADOW MOUSE

I

In a shoe box stuffed in an old nylon stocking
Sleeps the baby mouse I found in the meadow,
Where he trembled and shook beneath a stick
Till I caught him up by the tail and brought him in,
Cradled in my hand,
A little quaker, the whole body of him trembling,
His absurd whiskers sticking out like a cartoon-mouse,
His feet like small leaves,
Little lizard-feet,
Whitish and spread wide when he tried to struggle away,
Wriggling like a miniscule puppy.

Now he's eaten his three kinds of cheese and drunk from his
                                        bottle-cap watering-trough—
So much he just lies in one corner,
His tail curled under him, his belly big
As his head; his bat-like ears
Twitching, tilting toward the least sound.

Do I imagine he no longer trembles
When I come close to him?
He seems no longer to tremble.

II

But this morning the shoe-box house on the back porch is empty.
Where has he gone, my meadow mouse,
My thumb of a child that nuzzled in my palm?—
To run under the hawk's wing,

Under the eye of the great owl watching from the elm-tree,
To live by courtesy of the shrike, the snake, the tom-cat.

I think of the nestling fallen into the deep grass,
The turtle gasping in the dusty rubble of the highway,
The paralytic stunned in the tub, and the water rising,—
All things innocent, hapless, forsaken.

HEARD IN A VIOLENT WARD

In heaven, too,
You'd be institutionalized.
But that's all right,—
If they let you eat and swear
With the likes of Blake,
And Christopher Smart,
And that sweet man, John Clare.

THE GERANIUM

When I put her out, once, by the garbage pail,
She looked so limp and bedraggled,
So foolish and trusting, like a sick poodle,   *simile*
Or a wizened aster in late September,
I brought her back in again   *Personification*
For a new routine—
Vitamins, water, and whatever
Sustenance seemed sensible
At the time: she'd lived   *Person.*
So long on gin, bobbie pins, half-smoked cigars, dead beer,
Her shriveled petals falling
On the faded carpet, the stale
Steak grease stuck to her fuzzy leaves.
(Dried-out, she creaked like a tulip.)   *Simile*

The things she endured!—
The dumb dames shrieking half the night
Or the two of us, alone, both seedy,
Me breathing booze at her,
She leaning out of her pot toward the window.
                     Person
Near the end, she seemed almost to hear me— *Person.*
And that was scary—
So when that snuffling cretin of a maid
Threw her, pot and all, into the trash-can,
I said nothing.

But I sacked the presumptuous hag the next week,
I was that lonely.

ON THE QUAY

What they say on the quay is,
　'There's no shelter
From the blow of the wind,
　Or the sea's banter,—
There's two more to drown
　The week after.'

THE STORM
(Forio d'Ischia)

I

Against the stone breakwater,
Only an ominous lapping,
While the wind whines overhead,
Coming down from the mountain,
Whistling between the arbors, the winding terraces;
A thin whine of wires, a rattling and flapping of leaves,
And the small street-lamp swinging and slamming against the
lamp-pole.

Where have the people gone?
There is one light on the mountain.

II

Along the sea-wall, a steady sloshing of the swell,
The waves not yet high, but even,
Coming closer and closer upon each other;
A fine fume of rain driving in from the sea,
Riddling the sand, like a wide spray of buckshot,
The wind from the sea and the wind from the mountain contending,
Flicking the foam from the whitecaps straight upward into the
darkness.

A time to go home!—
And a child's dirty shift billows upward out of an alley,
A cat runs from the wind as we do,
Between the whitening trees, up Santa Lucia,
Where the heavy door unlocks,

[65]

And our breath comes more easy,—
Then a crack of thunder, and the black rain runs over us, over
The flat-roofed houses, coming down in gusts, beating
The walls, the slatted windows, driving
The last watcher indoors, moving the cardplayers closer
To their cards, their anisette.

III

We creep to our bed, and its straw mattress.
We wait; we listen.
The storm lulls off, then redoubles,
Bending the trees half-way down to the ground,
Shaking loose the last wizened oranges in the orchard,
Flattening the limber carnations.

A spider eases himself down from a swaying light-bulb,
Running over the coverlet, down under the iron bedstead.
The bulb goes on and off, weakly.
Water roars into the cistern.

We lie closer on the gritty pillow,
Breathing heavily, hoping—
For the great last leap of the wave over the breakwater,
The flat boom on the beach of the towering sea-swell,
The sudden shudder as the jutting sea-cliff collapses,
And the hurricane drives the dead straw into the living pine-tree.

THE THING

Suddenly they came flying, like a long scarf of smoke,
Trailing a thing—what was it?—small as a lark
Above the blue air, in the slight haze beyond,
A thing in and out of sight,
Flashing between gold levels of the late sun,
Then throwing itself up and away from the implacable swift
                                                              pursuers,
Confusing them once flying straight into the sun
So they circled aimlessly for almost a minute,
Only to find, with their long terrible eyes
The small thing diving down toward a hill,
Where they dropped again
In one streak of pursuit.

Then the first bird
Struck;
Then another, another,
Until there was nothing left,
Not even feathers from so far away.

And we turned to our picnic
Of veal soaked in marsala and little larks arranged on a long platter,
And we drank the dry harsh wine
While I poked with a stick at a stone near a four-pronged flower,
And a black bull nudged at a wall in the valley below,
And the blue air darkened.

THE PIKE

The river turns,
Leaving a place for the eye to rest,
A furred, a rocky pool,
A bottom of water.

The crabs tilt and eat, leisurely,
And the small fish lie, without shadow, motionless,
Or drift lazily in and out of the weeds.
The bottom-stones shimmer back their irregular striations,
And the half-sunken branch bends away from the gazer's eye.

A scene for the self to abjure!—
And I lean, almost into the water,
My eye always beyond the surface reflection;
I lean, and love these manifold shapes,
Until, out from a dark cove,
From beyond the end of a mossy log,
With one sinuous ripple, then a rush,
A thrashing-up of the whole pool,
The pike strikes.

ALL MORNING

Here in our aging district the wood pigeon lives with us,
His deep-throated cooing part of the early morning,
Far away, close-at-hand, his call floating over the on-coming traffic,
The lugubriously beautiful plaint uttered at regular intervals,
A protest from the past, a reminder.

They sit, three or four, high in the fir-trees back of the house,
Flapping away heavily when a car blasts too close,
And one drops down to the garden, the high rhododendron,
Only to fly over to his favorite perch, the cross-bar of a telephone
                                                                    pole;
Grave, hieratic, a piece of Assyrian sculpture,
A thing carved of stone or wood, with the dull iridescence of
                                                    long-polished wood,
Looking at you without turning his small head,
With a round vireo's eye, quiet and contained,
Part of the landscape.

And the Steller jay, raucous, sooty headed, lives with us,
Conducting his long wars with the neighborhood cats,
All during mating season,
Making a racket to wake the dead,
To distract attention from the short-tailed ridiculous young ones
Hiding deep in the blackberry bushes—
What a scuttling and rapping along the drainpipes,
A fury of jays, diving and squawking,
When our spayed female cat yawns and stretches out in the
                                                                sunshine—
And the wrens scold, and the chickadees frisk and frolic,
Pitching lightly over the high hedgerows, dee-deeing,
And the ducks near Lake Washington waddle down the highway
                                                    after a rain,

[69]

Stopping traffic, indignant as addled old ladies,
Pecking at crusts and peanuts, their green necks glittering;
And the hummingbird dips in and around the quince tree,
Veering close to my head,
Then whirring off sideways to the top of the hawthorn,
Its almost-invisible wings, buzzing, hitting the loose leaves
                                        intermittently—

A delirium of birds!
Peripheral dippers come to rest on the short grass,
Their heads jod-jodding like pigeons;
The gulls, the gulls far from their waves
Rising, wheeling away with harsh cries,
Coming down on a patch of lawn:

It is neither spring nor summer: it is Always,
With towhees, finches, chickadees, California quail, wood doves,
With wrens, sparrows, juncos, cedar waxwings, flickers,
With Baltimore orioles, Michigan bobolinks,
And those birds forever dead,
The passenger pigeon, the great auk, the Carolina paraquet,
All birds remembered, O never forgotten!
All in my yard, of a perpetual Sunday,
All morning! All morning!

THE MANIFESTATION

Many arrivals make us live: the tree becoming
Green, a bird tipping the topmost bough,
A seed pushing itself beyond itself,
The mole making its way through darkest ground,
The worm, intrepid scholar of the soil—
Do these analogies perplex? A sky with clouds,
The motion of the moon, and waves at play,
A sea-wind pausing in a summer tree.

What does what it should do needs nothing more.
The body moves, though slowly, toward desire.
We come to something without knowing why.

SONG

From whence cometh song?—
From the tear, far away,
From the hound giving tongue,
From the quarry's weak cry.

From whence, love?
From the dirt in the street,
From the bolt, stuck in its groove,
From the cur at my feet.

Whence, death?
From dire hell's mouth,
From the ghost without breath,
The wind shifting south.

THE TRANCED

I

We counted several flames in one small fire.
The question was, Where was the Questioner?—
When we abide yet go
Do we do more than we know,
Or is the body but a motion in a shoe?

II

The edge of heaven was sharper than a sword;
Divinity itself malign, absurd;
Yet love-longing of a kind
Rose up within the mind,
Rose up and fell like an erratic wind.

III

We struggled out of sensuality;
Going, we stayed; and night turned into day;
We paced the living ground;
The stones rang with light sound;
The leaves, the trees turned our two shapes around.

IV

Our eyes fixed on a point of light so fine
Subject and object sang and danced as one;
Slowly we moved between
The unseen and the seen,
Our bodies light, and lighted by the moon.

V

Our small souls hid from their small agonies,
Yet it's the nature of all love to rise:
Being, we came to be
Part of eternity,
And what died with us was the will to die.

THE MOMENT

We passed the ice of pain,
And came to a dark ravine,
And there we sang with the sea:
The wide, the bleak abyss
Shifted with our slow kiss.

Space struggled with time;
The gong of midnight struck
The naked absolute.
Sound, silence sang as one.

All flowed: without, within;
Body met body, we
Created what's to be.

What else to say?
We end in joy.

Sequence,
Sometimes Metaphysical

IN A DARK TIME

In a dark time, the eye begins to see,
I meet my shadow in the deepening shade;
I hear my echo in the echoing wood—
A lord of nature weeping to a tree.
I live between the heron and the wren,
Beasts of the hill and serpents of the den.

What's madness but nobility of soul
At odds with circumstance? The day's on fire!
I know the purity of pure despair,
My shadow pinned against a sweating wall.
That place among the rocks—is it a cave,
Or winding path? The edge is what I have.

A steady storm of correspondences!
A night flowing with birds, a ragged moon,
And in broad day the midnight come again!
A man goes far to find out what he is—
Death of the self in a long, tearless night,
All natural shapes blazing unnatural light.

Dark, dark my light, and darker my desire.
My soul, like some heat-maddened summer fly,
Keeps buzzing at the sill. Which I is I?
A fallen man, I climb out of my fear.
The mind enters itself, and God the mind,
And one is One, free in the tearing wind.

IN EVENING AIR

I

A dark theme keeps me here,
Though summer blazes in the vireo's eye.
Who would be half possessed
By his own nakedness?
Waking's my care—
I'll make a broken music, or I'll die.

II

Ye littles, lie more close!
Make me, O Lord, a last, a simple thing
Time cannot overwhelm.
Once I transcended time:
A bud broke to a rose,
And I rose from a last diminishing.

III

I look down the far light
And I behold the dark side of a tree
Far down a billowing plain,
And when I look again,
It's lost upon the night—
Night I embrace, a dear proximity.

IV

I stand by a low fire
Counting the wisps of flame, and I watch how
Light shifts upon the wall.
I bid stillness be still.
I see, in evening air,
How slowly dark comes down on what we do.

THE SEQUEL

I

Was I too glib about eternal things,
An intimate of air and all its songs?
Pure aimlessness pursued and yet pursued
And all wild longings of the insatiate blood
Brought me down to my knees. O who can be
Both moth and flame? The weak moth blundering by.
Whom do we love? I thought I knew the truth;
Of grief I died, but no one knew my death.

II

I saw a body dancing in the wind,
A shape called up out of my natural mind;
I heard a bird stir in its true confine;
A nestling sighed—I called that nestling mine;
A partridge drummed; a minnow nudged its stone;
We danced, we danced, under a dancing moon;
And on the coming of the outrageous dawn,
We danced together, we danced on and on.

III

Morning's a motion in a happy mind:
She stayed in light, as leaves live in the wind,
Swaying in air, like some long water weed.
She left my body, lighter than a seed;
I gave her body full and grave farewell.
A wind came close, like a shy animal.
A light leaf on a tree, she swayed away
To the dark beginnings of another day.

IV

Was nature kind? The heart's core tractable?
All waters waver, and all fires fail.
Leaves, leaves, lean forth and tell me what I am;
This single tree turns into purest flame.
I am a man, a man at intervals
Pacing a room, a room with dead-white walls;
I feel the autumn fail—all that slow fire
Denied in me, who has denied desire.

THE MOTION

I

The soul has many motions, body one.
An old wind-tattered butterfly flew down
And pulsed its wings upon the dusty ground—
Such stretchings of the spirit make no sound.
By lust alone we keep the mind alive,
And grieve into the certainty of love.

II

Love begets love. This torment is my joy.
I watch a river wind itself away;
To meet the world, I rise up in my mind;
I hear a cry and lose it on the wind.
What we put down, must we take up again?
I dare embrace. By striding, I remain.

III

Who but the loved know love's a faring-forth?
Who's old enough to live?—a thing of earth
Knowing how all things alter in the seed
Until they reach this final certitude,
This reach beyond this death, this act of love
In which all creatures share, and thereby live,

IV

Wings without feathers creaking in the sun,
The close dirt dancing on a sunless stone
God's night and day: down this space He has smiled,
O who would take the vision from the child?—
Hope has its hush: we move through its broad day,—
O, motion O, our chance is still to be!

INFIRMITY

In purest song one plays the constant fool
As changes shimmer in the inner eye.
I stare and stare into a deepening pool
And tell myself my image cannot die.
I love myself: that's my one constancy.
Oh, to be something else, yet still to be!

Sweet Christ, rejoice in my infirmity;
There's little left I care to call my own.
Today they drained the fluid from a knee
And pumped a shoulder full of cortisone;
Thus I conform to my divinity
By dying inward, like an aging tree.

The instant ages on the living eye;
Light on its rounds, a pure extreme of light
Breaks on me as my meager flesh breaks down—
The soul delights in that extremity.
Blessed the meek; they shall inherit wrath;
I'm son and father of my only death.

A mind too active is no mind at all;
The deep eye sees the shimmer on the stone;
The eternal seeks, and finds, the temporal,
The change from dark to light of the slow moon,
Dead to myself, and all I hold most dear,
I move beyond the reach of wind and fire.

Deep in the greens of summer sing the lives
I've come to love. A vireo whets its bill.
The great day balances upon the leaves;
My ears still hear the bird when all is still;
My soul is still my soul, and still the Son,
And knowing this, I am not yet undone.

[86]

Things without hands take hands: there is no choice,—
Eternity's not easily come by.
When opposites come suddenly in place,
I teach my eyes to hear, my ears to see
How body from spirit slowly does unwind
Until we are pure spirit at the end.

THE DECISION

I

What shakes the eye but the invisible?
Running from God's the longest race of all.
A bird kept haunting me when I was young—
The phoebe's slow retreating from its song,
Nor could I put that sound out of my mind,
The sleepy sound of leaves in a light wind.

II

Rising or falling's all one discipline!
The line of my horizon's growing thin!
Which is the way? I cry to the dread black,
The shifting shade, the cinders at my back.
Which is the way? I ask, and turn to go,
As a man turns to face on-coming snow.

THE MARROW

I

The wind from off the sea says nothing new.
The mist above me sings with its small flies.
From a burnt pine the sharp speech of a crow
Tells me my drinking breeds a will to die.
What's the worst portion in this mortal life?
A pensive mistress, and a yelping wife.

II

One white face shimmers brighter than the sun
When contemplation dazzles all I see;
One look too close can take my soul away.
Brooding on God, I may become a man.
Pain wanders through my bones like a lost fire;
What burns me now? Desire, desire, desire.

III

Godhead above my God, are you there still?
To sleep is all my life. In sleep's half-death,
My body alters, altering the soul
That once could melt the dark with its small breath.
Lord, hear me out, and hear me out this day:
From me to Thee's a long and terrible way.

IV

I was flung back from suffering and love
When light divided on a storm-tossed tree.
Yea, I have slain my will, and still I live;
I would be near; I shut my eyes to see;
I bleed my bones, their marrow to bestow
Upon that God who knows what I would know.

I WAITED

I waited for the wind to move the dust;
But no wind came.
I seemed to eat the air;
The meadow insects made a level noise.
I rose, a heavy bulk, above the field.

It was as if I tried to walk in hay,
Deep in the mow, and each step deeper down,
Or floated on the surface of a pond,
The slow long ripples winking in my eyes.
I saw all things through water, magnified,
And shimmering. The sun burned through a haze,
And I became all that I looked upon.
I dazzled in the dazzle of a stone.

And then a jackass brayed. A lizard leaped my foot.
Slowly I came back to the dusty road;
And when I walked, my feet seemed deep in sand.
I moved like some heat-weary animal.
I went, not looking back. I was afraid.

The way grew steeper between stony walls,
Then lost itself down through a rocky gorge.
A donkey path led to a small plateau.
Below, the bright sea was, the level waves,
And all the winds came toward me. I was glad.

THE TREE, THE BIRD

Uprose, uprose, the stony fields uprose,
And every snail dipped toward me its pure horn.
The sweet light met me as I walked toward
A small voice calling from a drifting cloud.
I was a finger pointing at the moon,
At ease with joy, a self-enchanted man.
Yet when I sighed, I stood outside my life,
A leaf unaltered by the midnight scene,
Part of a tree still dark, still, deathly still,
Riding the air, a willow with its kind,
Bearing its life and more, a double sound,
Kin to the wind, and the bleak whistling rain.

The willow with its bird grew loud, grew louder still.
I could not bear its song, that altering
With every shift of air, those beating wings,
The lonely buzz behind my midnight eyes;—
How deep the mother-root of that still cry!

The present falls, the present falls away;
How pure the motion of the rising day,
The white sea widening on a farther shore.
The bird, the beating bird, extending wings—.
Thus I endure this last pure stretch of joy,
The dire dimension of a final thing.

THE RESTORED

In a hand like a bowl
Danced my own soul,
Small as an elf,
All by itself.

When she thought I thought
She dropped as if shot.
'I've only one wing,' she said,
'The other's gone dead.'

'I'm maimed; I can't fly;
I'm like to die,'
Cried the soul
From my hand like a bowl.

When I raged, when I wailed,
And my reason failed,
That delicate thing
Grew back a new wing,

And danced, at high noon,
On a hot, dusty stone,
In the still point of light
Of my last midnight.

THE RIGHT THING

Let others probe the mystery if they can.
Time-harried prisoners of *Shall* and *Will*—
The right thing happens to the happy man.

The bird flies out, the bird flies back again;
The hill becomes the valley, and is still;
Let others delve that mystery if they can.

God bless the roots!—Body and soul are one!
The small become the great, the great the small;
The right thing happens to the happy man.

Child of the dark, he can out leap the sun,
His being single, and that being all:
The right thing happens to the happy man.

Or he sits still, a solid figure when
The self-destructive shake the common wall;
Takes to himself what mystery he can,

And, praising change as the slow night comes on,
Wills what he would, surrendering his will
Till mystery is no more: No more he can.
The right thing happens to the happy man.

ONCE MORE, THE ROUND

What's greater, Pebble or Pond?
What can be known? The Unknown.
My true self runs toward a Hill
More! O More! visible.

Now I adore my life
With the Bird, the abiding Leaf,
With the Fish, the questing Snail,
And the Eye altering all;
And I dance with William Blake
For love, for Love's sake;

And everything comes to One,
As we dance on, dance on, dance on.